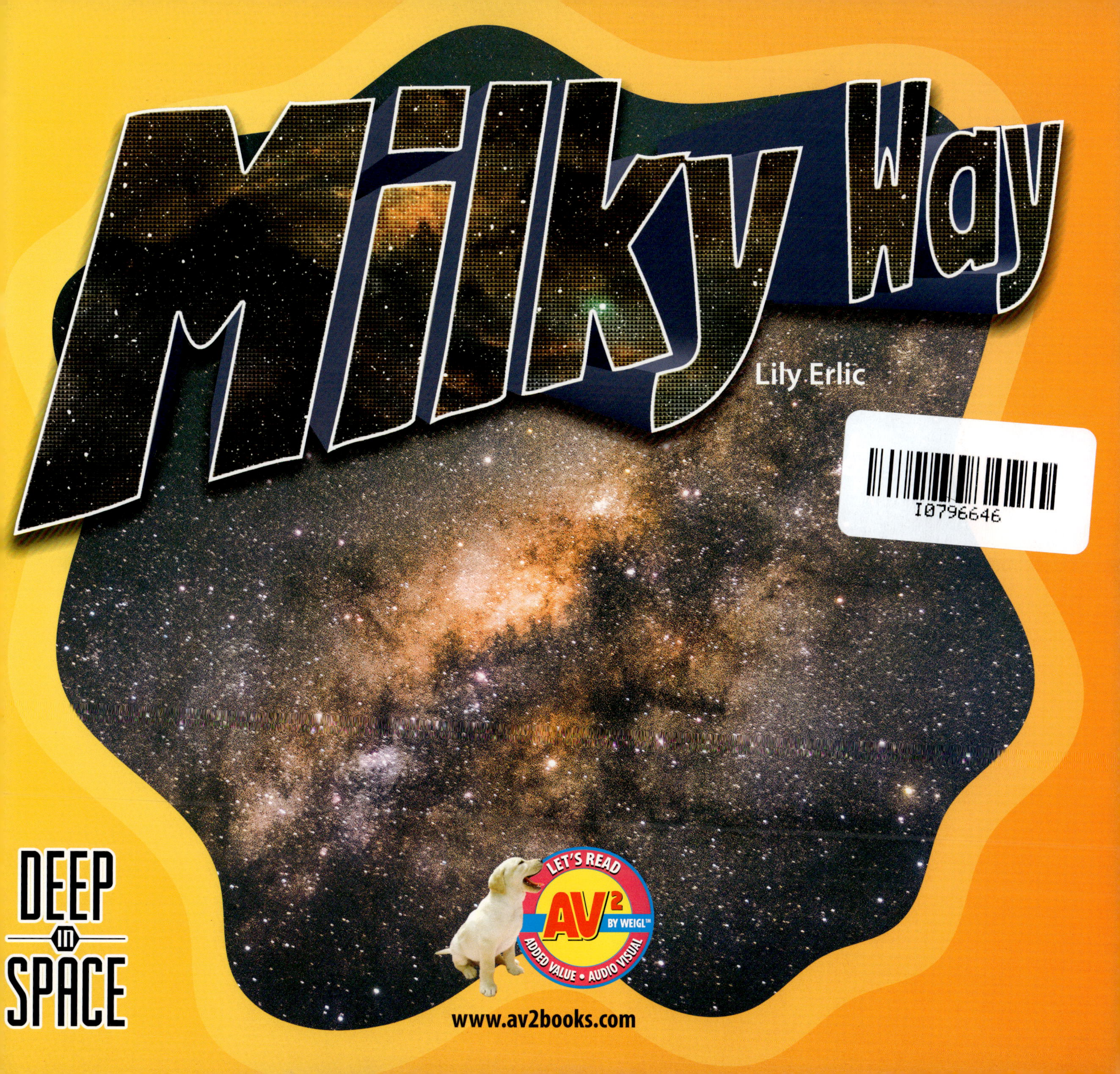
Milky Way
Lily Erlic
I0796646
DEEP
in
SPACE
LET'S READ
AV2
BY WEIGL™
ADDED VALUE • AUDIO VISUAL
www.av2books.com

Go to www.av2books.com, and enter this book's unique code.

BOOK CODE

AVP69296

AV² by Weigl brings you media enhanced books that support active learning.

AV² provides enriched content that supplements and complements this book. Weigl's AV² books strive to create inspired learning and engage young minds in a total learning experience.

Your AV² Media Enhanced books come alive with...

Audio
Listen to sections of the book read aloud.

Video
Watch informative video clips.

Embedded Weblinks
Gain additional information for research.

Try This!
Complete activities and hands-on experiments.

Key Words
Study vocabulary, and complete a matching word activity.

Quizzes
Test your knowledge.

Slideshow
View images and captions, and prepare a presentation.

... and much, much more!

Published by AV² by Weigl
350 5th Avenue, 59th Floor
New York, NY 10118
Website: www.av2books.com

Library of Congress Control Number: 2019941867

ISBN 978-1-7911-0958-5 (hardcover)
ISBN 978-1-7911-0959-2 (softcover)
ISBN 978-1-7911-0960-8 (multi-user eBook)

Printed in Guangzhou, China
1 2 3 4 5 6 7 8 9 0 23 22 21 20 19

052019
102918

Project Coordinator: John Willis
Designer: Terry Paulhus

Every reasonable effort has been made to trace ownership and to obtain permission to reprint copyright material. The publishers would be pleased to have any errors or omissions brought to their attention so that they may be corrected in subsequent printings.

Weigl acknowledges Alamy, Getty Images, Shutterstock, and Wikimedia as its primary image suppliers for this title.

CONTENTS

The Milky Way is a galaxy. A galaxy is made of dust, gas, and billions of stars.

People on Earth can see the Milky Way if they are far from city lights.

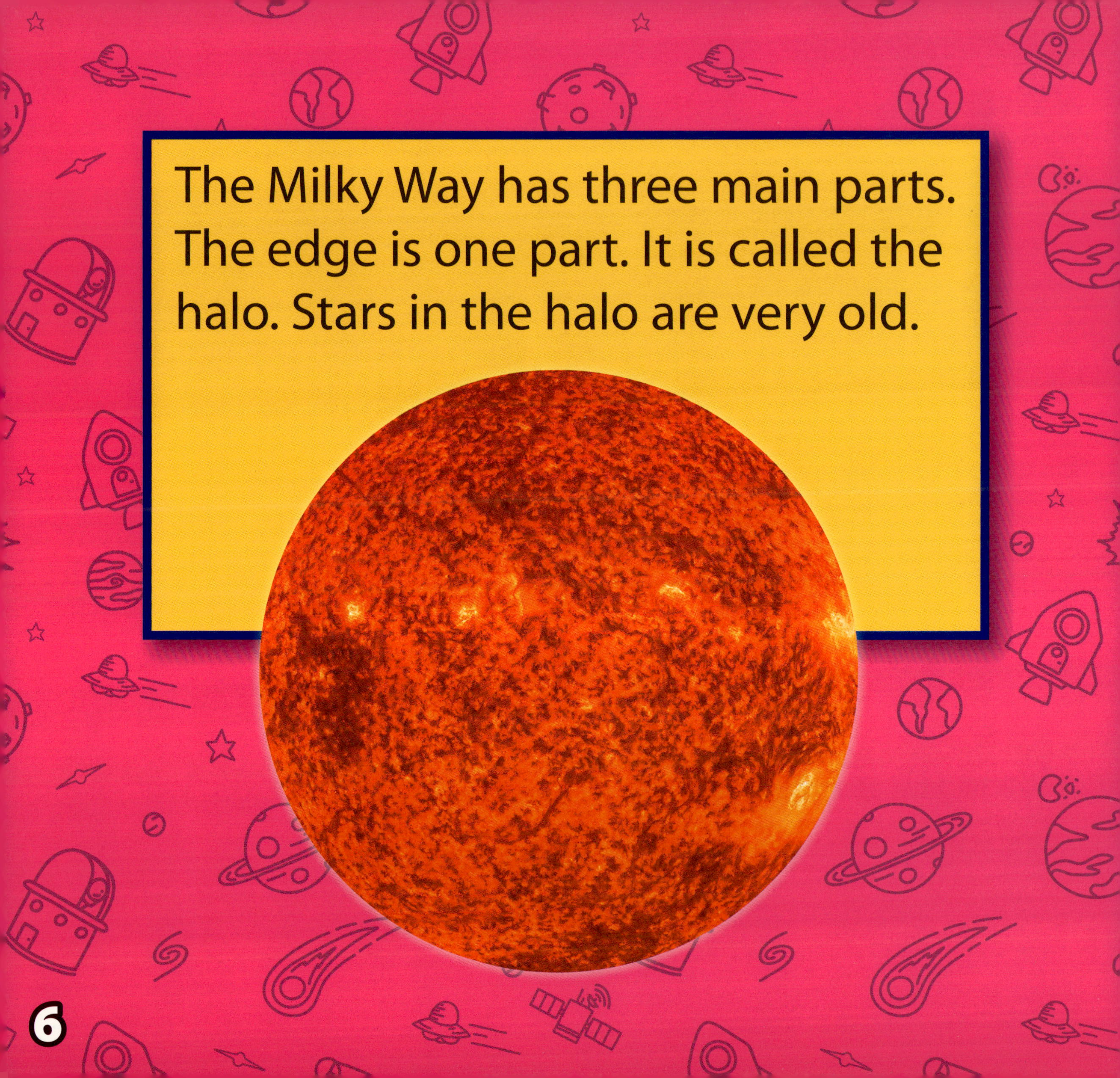

The Milky Way has three main parts. The edge is one part. It is called the halo. Stars in the halo are very old.

Halo

The disk is the biggest part of the Milky Way. It has many stars.

Disk

The disk is made up of spiral arms.
They give the Milky Way its shape.

Another part of the Milky Way is the bulge. It is near the Milky Way's center.

Bulge

The bulge looks like a football. It has gas, dust, and many stars.

Scientists think there is a black hole in the center of the Milky Way. All of the stars in the galaxy move around it.

Saturn
Mercury
Venus
Earth
Mars
Jupiter

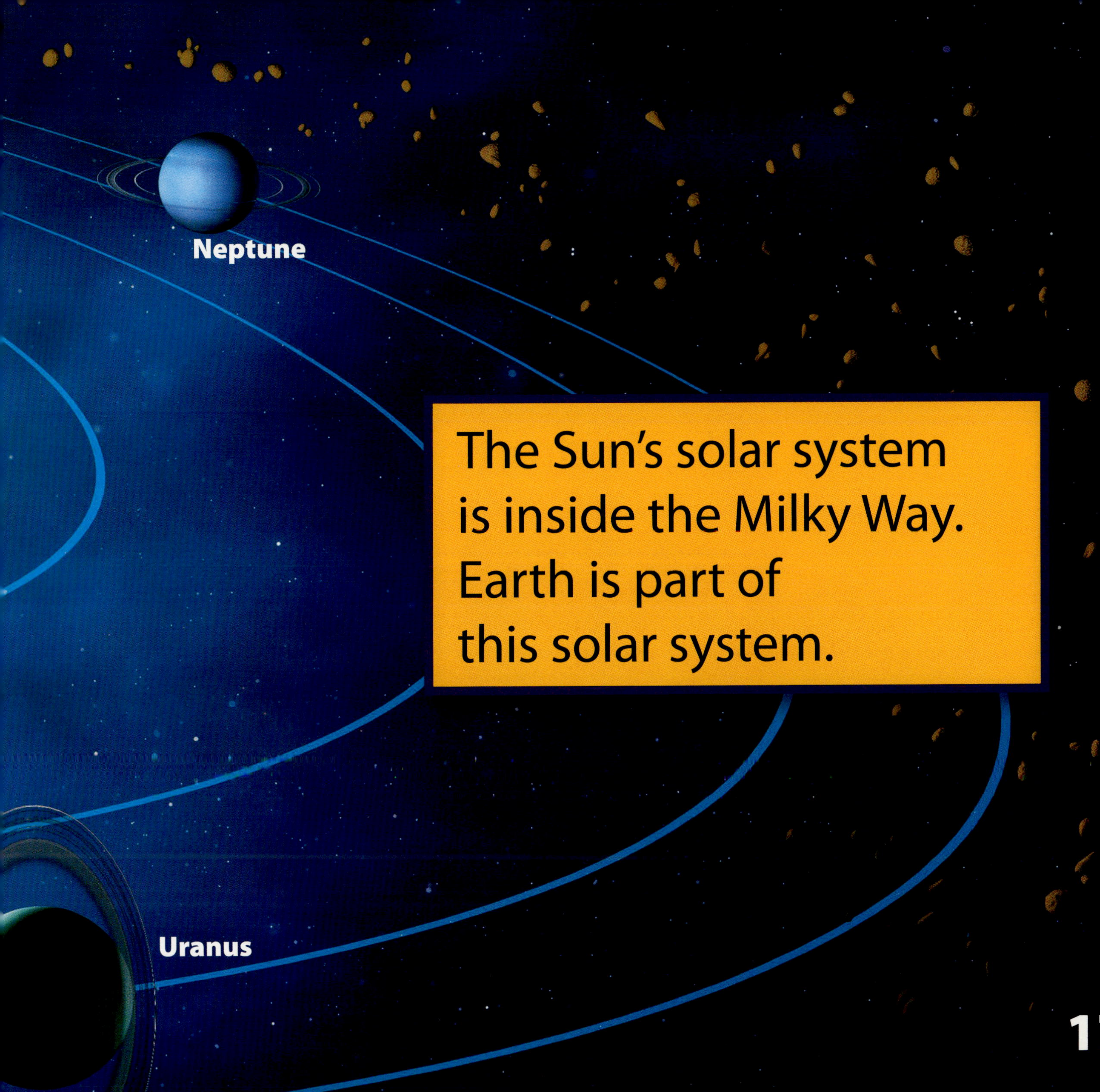

The Sun's solar system is inside the Milky Way. Earth is part of this solar system.

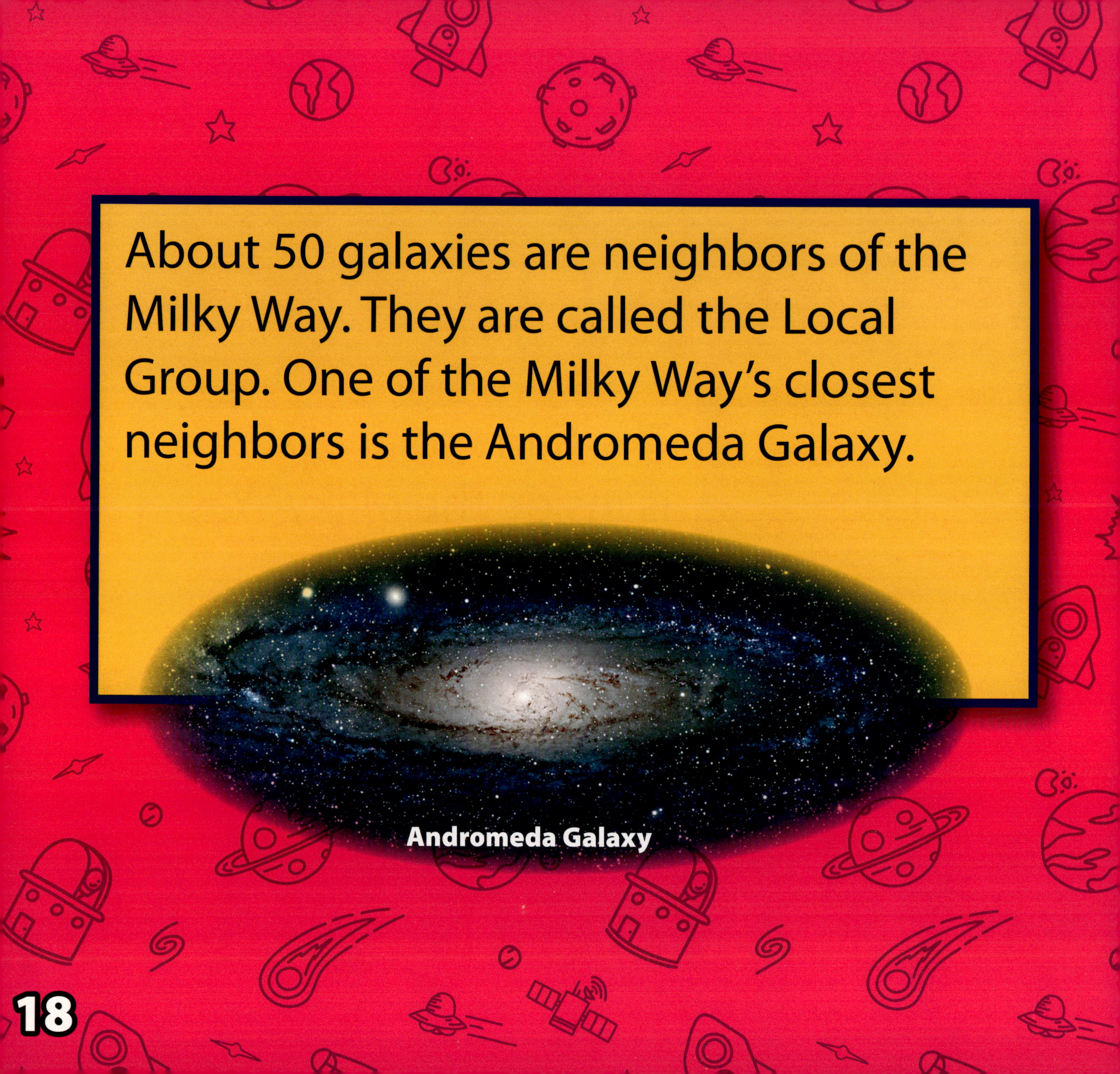

About 50 galaxies are neighbors of the Milky Way. They are called the Local Group. One of the Milky Way's closest neighbors is the Andromeda Galaxy.

Andromeda Galaxy

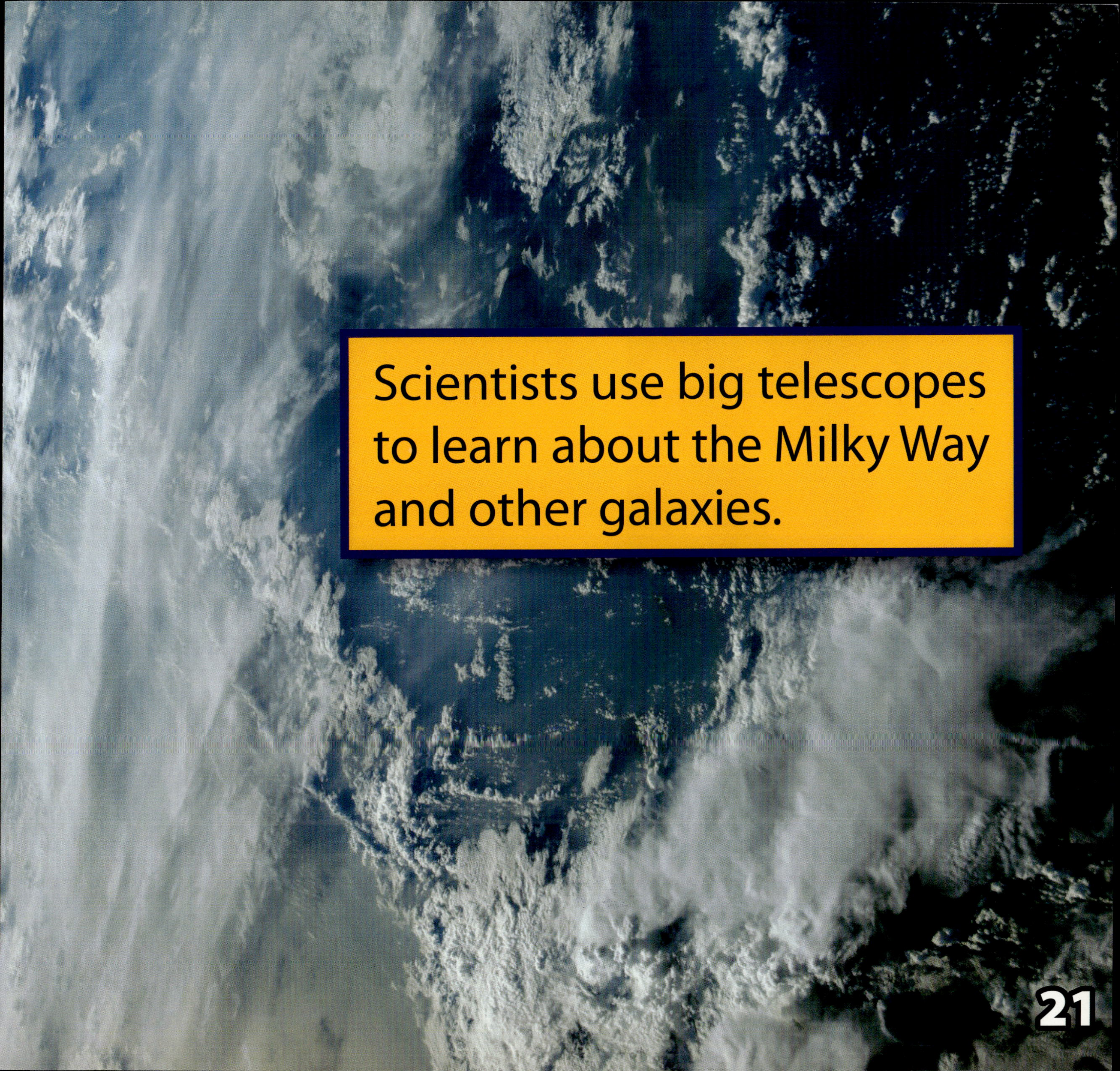

Scientists use big telescopes to learn about the Milky Way and other galaxies.

MILKY WAY FACTS

These pages provide detailed information that expands on the interesting facts found in the book. They are intended to be used by adults as a learning support to help young readers round out their knowledge of each object or event featured in the *Deep in Space* series.

Pages 4–5

The Milky Way is a galaxy. On dark nights, people can see the Milky Way. It looks like a white band of spilled milk. The Milky Way's many stars make it sparkle like glitter. Humans can only see about 5,000 of them. The Milky Way is a barred spiral galaxy. Spiral galaxies are round. They have long spiral arms. The spiral arms move in a circle around the center.

Pages 6–7

The Milky Way has three main parts. The stars in the halo are old and contain dark matter. Dark matter is an unknown material found in space. It is invisible, but scientists know that it exists. There are about 150 globular clusters in the halo. Globular clusters are groups of stars. From far away, they look like piles of glitter.

Pages 8–9

The disk is the biggest part of the Milky Way. The disk is in the middle of the Milky Way. It is oval and appears flat from above. Most of the Milky Way's stars are found there. The stars in the disk all move around the center of the Milky Way in the same direction. They travel about 540,000 miles (869,045 kilometers) per hour.

Pages 10–11

The disk is made up of spiral arms. Scientists learn more about the Milky Way every day. They believe there are four main spiral arms and several smaller arms. The main arms are called Orion-Cygnus, Carina-Sagittarius, Scutum-Centaurus, and Perseus. Each arm holds billions of stars and planets. Earth is located on the Orion-Cygnus arm.

Pages 12–13

Another part of the Milky Way is the bulge. There is a galactic bar at the center of the bulge. The bulge is about 13,000 light years across. Each light year is equal to 6 trillion miles (10 trillion kilometers). There are about 10 million stars in the bulge. There are so many stars in the bulge that it is hard to see from one side to the other.

Pages 14–15

Scientists think there is a black hole in the center of the Milky Way. A black hole pulls objects inside of itself. Objects that move near the black hole, such as stars, are sucked up as if by a vacuum. Black holes are invisible, but scientists can see flares when hot gas goes into the black hole. The black hole in the center of the Milky Way is about 4.31 million times bigger than the Sun.

Pages 16–17

The Sun's solar system is inside the Milky Way. A solar system is a group of planets with a star at the center. The Sun's solar system is located halfway between the edge of the Milky Way and its center. It contains eight planets. Astronomers believe there could be billions of other solar systems in the universe.

Pages 18–19

About 50 galaxies are neighbors of the Milky Way. Scientists say there could be 2 trillion more galaxies in the universe. Andromeda is similar to the Milky Way galaxy. It is also a spiral galaxy. Astronomers think that Andromeda may crash into the Milky Way in about 4.5 billion years. When this happens, they will form a new galaxy.

Pages 20–21

Scientists use big telescopes to learn about the Milky Way and other galaxies. The Hubble Space Telescope takes pictures of objects in space. It has taken more than 1.5 million pictures of stars, planets, and the Sun. Hubble helps scientists learn about how objects in space are formed. The telescope is solar-powered, which means the Sun makes it work.

KEY WORDS

Research has shown that as much as 65 percent of all written material published in English is made up of 300 words. These 300 words cannot be taught using pictures or learned by sounding them out. They must be recognized by sight. This book contains 46 common sight words to help young readers improve their reading fluency and comprehension. This book also teaches young readers several important content words, such as proper nouns. These words are paired with pictures to aid in learning and improve understanding.

Page	Sight Words First Appearance
4	a, and, is, made, of, the
5	are, can, city, Earth, far, from, if, lights, on, people, see, they
6	has, in, old, one, parts, three, very
9	it, many
10	give, its, up
12	another, near
13	like, looks
15	all, around, move, there, think
17	this
18	about
21	big, learn, other, to, use

Page	Content Words First Appearance
4	dust, galaxy, gas, Milky Way, stars
6	edge, halo
9	disk
10	spiral arms
12	bulge
13	football
15	black hole, scientists
16	Jupiter, Mars, Mercury, Saturn, Venus
17	Neptune, solar system, Sun, Uranus
18	Andromeda Galaxy, Local Group, neighbors
21	telescopes